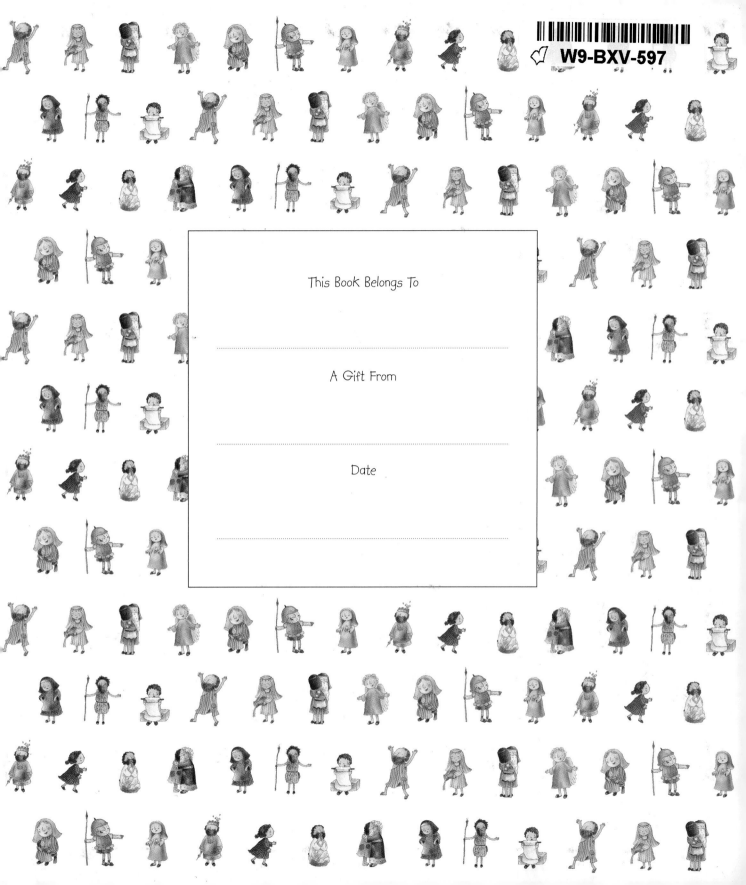

This Book Belongs To

....

A Gift From

....

Date

....

Published in the UK by Hodder & Stoughton
An Hachette Livre Company
ISBN 978 0340 979 204

First edition 2008

Copyright © 2008 Anno Domini Publishing
1 Churchgates, The Wilderness, Berkhamsted, Herts HP4 2UB England
Text copyright © 2008 Jan Godfrey
Illustrations copyright © 2008 Paola Bertolini Grudina

Editorial Director Annette Reynolds
Editor Nicola Bull
Art Director Gerald Rogers
Pre-production Krystyna Kowalska Hewitt
Production John Laister

A CIP catalogue record for this title is available from the British Library.

Printed and bound in Singapore

MY FIRST
BIBLE

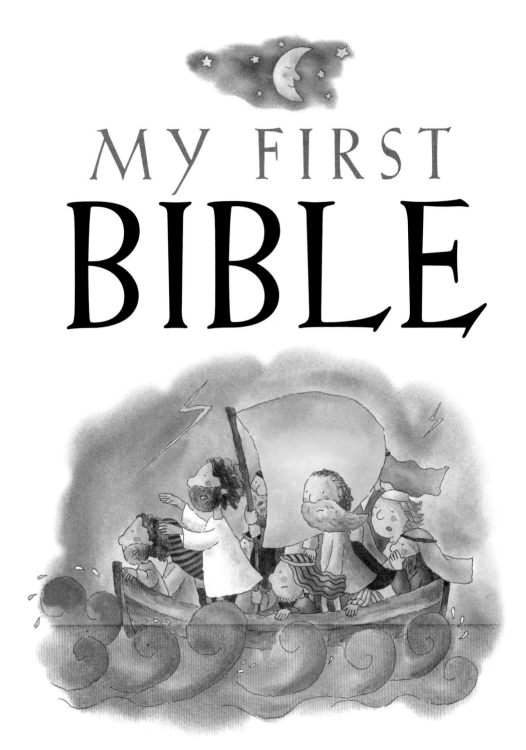

Jan Godfrey and Paola Bertolini Grudina

C O N T

E N T S

God made the world

Long, long, ago, at the beginning of time, God said, 'Let there be light,' and bright, shining light shone in the darkness.

God said, 'Let there be land and sea,' and there was wide land and tall mountains and deep, wet water in the sea.

God said, 'Let there be trees and plants, sun, moon and stars,' and so the plants produced juicy fruits in the hot sunshine. At night they were cool under the silver moon and twinkly stars.

God said, 'Let there be fish and all sorts of winged creatures,' and the sea swam with fish and the sky was filled with birds and butterflies.

God said, 'Let there be all kinds of animals,' and snakes slithered and giraffes galloped over the land. Monkeys swung through the trees and hippos

bathed in the rivers.

God said, 'Now let there be people to look after my beautiful world,' and there were.

God looked at his beautiful creation and saw that it was good. Then he rested.

Noah builds a boat

God told Noah it was going to rain very, very hard. Hammer, hammer, bang, bang! Noah built a boat, a very, very big boat called an ark.

God told Noah to take his family and all the animals into the

ark. Plod, plod, clip, clop! They went into the ark two by two by two by two.

Once God had closed the door of the ark, the rain started to fall. Splish, splash, splosh, splush!

The water covered the ground. The water covered the trees. The water covered the mountain tops. But the ark bobbed about on the waves, with Noah and the animals safe inside.

Days and days and days passed before the rain stopped raining.

Noah opened a window to set free a dove. Flap, flap, coo, coo! At last, the dove came back with a leaf in its beak.

God told Noah it was safe for his family and all the animals to come out of the ark. Then God sent a beautiful rainbow.

'There will never be a flood like this again,' God promised.

Under the stars

A very long time ago, a rich man called Abraham lived in a big city called Ur.

God told Abraham he was to leave Ur. Instead, he was to go from place to place, living in a tent, until God gave him a new home.

Abraham trusted God. He knew it would be a difficult journey. It was. Abraham and his wife Sarah travelled across dry, rocky hills. It was hard for them both. It was hard for their servants and sheep and goats.

'Come and look at the stars,' God said to Abraham one dark and twinkly night. 'You are just the beginning. There will be many, many people in your family. There will be many, many children born to the people in your family. There will be many, many – just like the stars you see in the sky.'

Abraham was puzzled. They had no children and they were getting old. However could this be?

But Abraham knew God. He knew that God always keeps his promises.

Three visitors

One sunny day, three visitors came to Abraham and Sarah as they sat in the shade near their tent.

This was a surprise. It was very hot for travelling.

'Here's water for washing and drinking,' said Abraham. Then he served them a meal that Sarah cooked for them. They ate bread and meat and cream and milk under the cool trees.

Sarah stayed in the tent. She hid there and listened to the men talking.

'You will have a child quite soon,' said one of the men to Abraham. 'Sarah will give birth to a baby boy.'

Sarah laughed out loud.

'I'm much too old to have a baby!' she giggled. 'I'm old enough to be a grandma!'

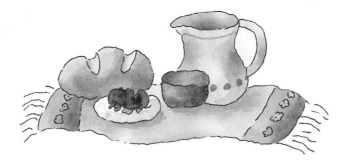

'Why did you laugh?' asked the visitor.

'I didn't – not really,' said Sarah, feeling rather silly.

'Oh yes, you did!' said the visitor. 'But nothing is too hard for God to do. You wait and see.'

Then Abraham knew that the visitors were like angels from God, and that Sarah would have a son.

So they did wait, and they did see, because one day quite soon, Sarah's baby boy was born. His name was Isaac.

Isaac and Rebecca

When Isaac was grown up, his father Abraham wanted to find a good wife for him to marry. So he sent his servant on a long journey back to his home country to find one. The servant took with him ten camels.

When they stopped by a well, the servant asked God to send a girl who would be willing to bring water for him – and for his ten thirsty camels! Such a girl must be a good wife for Isaac.

The servant watched as a beautiful girl called Rebecca came to speak to him.

'Would you like some water?' she asked him. 'Can I water your camels too?'

Rebecca was very
surprised when the
servant gave her two
gold bracelets! The
servant met her
family and found
they were related to
Abraham. He gave them presents
as well. He knew that God had
sent him to the right place.

Then he took Rebecca on
the long journey back with him to
Abraham.

Isaac was out in the fields
when he saw Rebecca and the
camels coming towards him in the
distance. Isaac knew that he loved
her and wanted her to be his wife.

Joseph and his brothers

Joseph had a beautiful coat. It was a present from his father Jacob.

Joseph had eleven brothers, too.

'Grumble, grumble, not fair, not fair,' they said. They were very jealous of him.

Joseph had strange dreams. He dreamed about the sun and the moon and the stars. They bowed down to his star! He dreamed about bundles of corn that his brothers had grown. They all bowed down to Joseph's own bundles of corn!

'Grumble, grouch, think you're special do you?' muttered his brothers. 'Think we'll bow down to you, do you? Huh! Ha!'

They were so angry that they threw Joseph into a deep, dark pit. Then they dragged him out and sold him to some traders – just as if he were a goat or a basket of fruit!

They pretended a wild animal had killed him and Joseph's father was very, very sad.

But God looked after Joseph.

First, he was taken to Egypt. Then he worked for a kind master. Then he was put in prison. Then he was a slave. Then... he was taken to see the King of Egypt!

Dreams come true

The King of Egypt had strange dreams, and he was told that Joseph could help him.

'I saw seven thin, skinny cows eat up seven plump, fat cows!' said the King. 'Moo, moo, moo, moo, moo, moo, moo! Moo, moo, moo, moo, moo, moo, moo.'

'Then I saw seven parched, dry ears of corn eat up seven plump, ripe ears of corn!'

'It means there'll be seven years when there's plenty to eat,' said Joseph. 'Then there'll be seven years when there'll be nothing to eat at all!'

Then Joseph became an important person, almost as important as the King of Egypt himself. He helped people store up lots and lots and lots of corn.

The people of Egypt did not go hungry, but Joseph's family in Canaan were very hungry indeed. Soon Joseph's brothers came to buy corn. They bowed low before Joseph.

Joseph remembered how jealous they had been of him. Joseph remembered the horrible things they had done to him. Joseph remembered the first dream he had when the sun and moon and stars bowed down to him – and he knew that God had made everything good again.

'I am your brother,' said Joseph. 'Bring my father here so we can all be together again – and have plenty to eat!'

Little baby Moses

'Waahhh!' cried little baby Moses. 'Waahhh!'
    Moses' mum was terribly afraid that the King or his soldiers would hear him crying. And as he grew bigger, his tears grew bigger and he cried even more loudly:
    'WAAHHH!'
    'WAAHHH!'
    'WAAHHH!'

'Oh dear,' said Moses' mum. 'I wish you wouldn't cry so loudly. The King doesn't like baby boys one little bit. He doesn't like baby boys at all because they grow up into men who might fight him. He mustn't hear you crying. He might get so angry that he will kill you!'

Then Moses' mum had a very good idea. She wove some reeds together with sticky tar. She made a basket safe to float on the water and lay baby Moses inside.

'Go and watch,' said Moses' mum to Moses' big sister Miriam.

Miriam hid by the river and watched her baby brother bobbing about in the basket. First he chuckled and cooed. Then he cried...

'WAAHHH!'

And who should come along but the King's own daughter!

'Oh!' said the princess. 'A baby! I'll look after you, little baby.'

'I'll find a nurse to help you,' said Miriam. And she fetched her own mum, baby Moses' mum!

Now everyone was happy. And God had kept baby Moses safe.

The king who said 'No!'

Moses grew up to be a great leader of his people.

One day, God's voice called to him out of a bright and blazing bush.

'You, Moses, are going to lead my people out of Egypt to a better country,' said God.

'Oh no I'm not,' said Moses hastily, afraid. He shivered in his shoes.

'Oh yes you are,' said God firmly. 'And take those shoes off. This ground where you're standing is holy and special. You are going to make the King of Egypt let my people go. But I promise I will help you.'

'OK, God,' sighed Moses. 'I'll do as you ask.'

After that, all sorts of things happened.

'Let my people go,' said Moses to the King of Egypt. But the King of Egypt wouldn't listen.

So... the rivers went muddy. Yuk! There was no fresh water.

There were frogs and gnats and flies everywhere, hopping and humming and buzzing.

Animals and people fell ill.

Huge hailstones rained down from the dark sky.

Clouds of insects came chewing and chomping at the crops until the ground was bare.

'Let my people go!' said Moses to the King. But still the king said, 'No!'

Finally, when every first-born child and animal had died, Moses led his people away from Egypt.

Follow-my-leader

Every day, a tall cloud showed Moses and the people where to go. Every night, a tall fire showed them where to rest.

When they reached the Red Sea, Moses lifted his special wooden stick and the wind blew. The water flowed to either side, and everyone crossed over.

God provided food called manna when the people were hungry. It appeared on the ground early in the morning and tasted sweet like honey.

God provided water when they were thirsty. Moses touched a rock with his special wooden stick

– and clean water flowed.

The people grumbled day by day. The people followed Moses day by day. And Moses followed God day by day.

One day, Moses went and talked with God high on a mountain. The mountain thundered and rumbled, the mountain puffed and smoked and the people were afraid. But when Moses came down from the mountain, he brought with him God's rules for living – ten special rules to help them to be happy.

The best way to live

God gave Moses ten special rules written on two big stones. The rules were to make us and other people happy and to help us live good lives.

'I am the true and living God,' said God. 'Don't worship any other gods but me.

'Don't worship pictures or statues of me. I am much greater than any beautiful picture or statue.

'And don't use my name wrongly,' said God. 'My name is special and holy. Treat it with respect.

'The seventh day of the week is special,' said God. 'It's a rest day, a family day, a happy day, a holy day. It's a day when everyone can worship me together. Even the animals can have a rest!

'Look after your mums and dads,' said God. 'Be polite and loving and respectful and kind and obedient to them.

'And don't hurt anyone, or even think about hurting them. Don't kill anyone.

'Don't take someone else's wife or husband and treat them as if they are your own wife or husband.

'Don't steal from people or take anything that belongs to them without asking first.

'And don't tell lies – or say nasty things about other people.

'Don't look at the things other people have and want them so much that you can't think about anything else.'

'Here you are,' said Moses to all the people. 'This is what God has said. This is the best way to live and be happy. Now we need to obey him.'

Joshua's big battle

When Moses died, Joshua led the people. God told Joshua to be brave and to trust him – because he was going to take Joshua and his people into the land where he'd promised they should live.

First they had to cross the River Jordan – wide and fast and deep and dangerous.

'The living God is with us,' Joshua told the people. 'Don't be afraid!'

As the priests stepped into the river, it dried up! Everyone was able to cross safely and make their way towards the city of Jericho.

Then they had to get past the city walls – tall and thick and high and wide.

'God will give us the city,' said

Joshua. 'Don't be afraid!'

Joshua sent his soldiers to march around the city walls, once, twice, three, four, five, six and seven times. The priests blew their trumpets – very NOISILY and very LOUDLY and everybody SHOUTED! Then... CRASH! The walls of the city fell down!

Joshua and God's people won the battle of Jericho and were able to live in Canaan, the land that God had promised them.

Gideon's good friend, God

Gideon was a good man, but he was afraid of his enemies. The Midianites swept down on their camels and took all the food that God's people were growing. Gideon hid so they would not find him.

Then God sent an angel to visit him.

'Hello, you strong, brave man!' said the angel. 'God wants you to help his people.'

Gideon looked around him to see who the angel could be talking to. Surely it wasn't him?

'People have stopped worshipping God. That's why your enemies are taking your food and making your lives difficult. God wants you to stop them.'

'But I am no one! I am not big or clever or special and my family is not big or clever or special... If God really wants me to help, I need him to show me he really means me!'

God heard Gideon. One day, he made Gideon's woollen fleece

wet when the ground around was dry and another day he made Gideon's woollen fleece dry when the ground was wet with dew.

Then Gideon knew that God had chosen him to help his people. He trusted God and did all that God told him – and the Midianites were driven away. The Israelites could live safely again.

Ruth in the cornfield

Ruth was kind and good. Naomi was old and sad.

Ruth went to Naomi's faraway country so Naomi would not be sad. The country was strange. The country was new.

'You're like my own mother,' said Ruth. 'I will stay with you and your people in your country, and I will worship the same true God.'

Ruth worked in the cornfield so there would be food for them both. Boaz, who owned the cornfield, was kind and good. He offered to look after Ruth and made sure she had enough food to take home to Naomi.

'God is kind and good!' said Naomi. 'He has sent us here to Boaz, who is one of our own family!'

Boaz could see that Ruth was kind and good. He wanted to marry Ruth. First, he made sure that no one else would mind. Then he made sure Ruth would be happy to marry him. Then Boaz married Ruth, and they were very happy together. They had a baby boy called Obed.

Naomi was still old, but she wasn't sad any more. She was happy to be part of Ruth's family and to hold her little grandchild.

The voice in the night

Long, long ago there lived a lady called Hannah. She wanted a baby of her very own.

'Please help me,' Hannah prayed to God. 'I do so want a baby, and any child I have will be yours as well.'

At last, God gave Hannah a baby boy, and she took him to the temple. She was very, very happy.

'Thank you, God,' said Hannah.

'I will look after Samuel,' said the old priest Eli. 'I'll teach him about God. I'll teach him the right way to live. I'll be kind to him.'

One night, Samuel was sleeping when he heard someone calling his name.

'Samuel!'

Samuel ran to old Eli.

'Here I am,' said Samuel.

'I didn't call you,' said Eli. 'Go back to bed.'

Then Samuel heard someone calling his name – again.

'Samuel!'

Once... twice... Samuel ran to Eli – again.

'Here I am,' said Samuel – again.

'I didn't call you,' said Eli – again. 'Go back to bed.'

So Samuel went back to bed – again.

Then he heard his name called again.

'Samuel!'

Once... twice... three times.

This time Eli knew it was God calling Samuel.

'Tell God you're listening to him,' said Eli.

'I'm listening, God,' said Samuel. 'I will always listen to you.'

Seven sons and a shepherd boy

Who would be the next King?

Samuel asked God to help him choose the right person.

At a party, a man called Jesse brought seven of his sons to Samuel. They stood before Samuel one by one.

'Should it be the tallest and strongest?' thought Samuel. One... two... three... four... five... six ... seven. All of them were tall and strong.

Then God whispered in Samuel's ear very quietly.

'Not the tallest, not the strongest. Only the person who's good and true inside is the person I have chosen to be the King.'

Samuel thought hard and asked, 'Haven't you any other sons?'

'Well, there's David,' said Jesse. 'But he's only a young lad, a shepherd boy, and he's out in the fields with the sheep right now.'

'I'll wait,' said Samuel. 'Send him to me.'

David came in, healthy and happy from the fields. Samuel looked him up and down.

'This is the boy God has chosen to be king,' said Samuel. 'Not the tallest, not the strongest, but the person who's good and true inside.'

He sprinkled a few drops of oil on David's head as his brothers looked on. David knew that God would always be there to help him.

David and Goliath

David, the shepherd boy, was not very big. The enemy, Goliath, was very, very LARGE. He was HUGE. He was ENORMOUS. He was VAST.

He was GINORMOUS. He was a GIANT!

Goliath's army stood on one side smiling. King Saul's army stood on the other side looking very worried indeed.

Goliath came striding towards King Saul's army. He was wearing a lot of heavy armour. He looked very ugly and fierce and full of badness. Everyone was very, very afraid of him.

'I'll go out and fight him,' said David. 'God helped me fight lions and bears when I looked after my sheep. He will help me now.'

King Saul lent David his very heavy armour. But the armour was so heavy he could hardly move. David took it off again.

'YOU?!' roared the giant. 'Who are YOU?!'

David found five pebbles in the stream, one... two... three... four... five. He whirled one around in his sling.

Then... wham!

Goliath fell to the ground. And that was the end of him – the big, bold giant who was full of badness.

King Saul's army cheered and shouted. Goliath's army turned... and ran away!

David the song-writer

King David wrote a lot of songs. Some of his songs were happy and some were sad. Some were brave and some were bold. Some were praises and some were prayers.

King David often wrote songs about God. In some David said how great God was. In others David asked God to help him. David told God everything, because God was David's friend.

David knew that God was always with him when he felt happy, and sang and danced and shouted Alleluia for joy. He knew that God was always with him when he felt sad and frightened and cross and lonely and grumpy.

One of the songs he wrote was about God being like a good shepherd. It's a special song called a psalm.

'The Lord's my shepherd, and I'm his sheep;
he leads me where it's rough and steep,
or by still waters, cool and deep.
He walks beside me every day,
in all the places where I play;
in every step along the way.
I walk behind him in his light,

in the darkness shining bright;
I know I'm always in his sight.
He spreads out food and comes to greet –
"Everybody, take a seat!
Everybody, come and eat!"'

Solomon

Young King Solomon had a dream one night.

'What would you like me to give you?' asked God.

Solomon thought hard. Did he want to be rich and great and have lots of money? Did he want to be famous and strong and brave? Did he want lots of things for himself?

Then Solomon answered God.

'I think really I'd like to be good and wise, fair and just and true – a really good and obedient King. I'd like to rule my people well.'

'Good,' said God. 'Excellent. That's great. You shall be a good and wise King, and a lot more besides.'

King Solomon was a good and wise King. All sorts of people came to him. He told them things that were good and true and helpful. He taught them how to live a good and happy life.

Then King Solomon built a great and wonderful temple for

God. It was made of gold and silver and wood and stones and iron and bronze and jewels with many, many beautifully carved decorations.

'This temple building is a place for your people to come and pray to you and tell you how great you are,' said Solomon. 'But I know that you are with us, God, wherever we are.'

Elijah and the ravens

'It's not going to rain for a very long time,' said Elijah to King Ahab. 'God has said so. He's not at all happy with the bad things you have been doing.

'There won't be much to eat. There won't be much to drink. Nothing will grow and the earth will be dry and bare.'

'Mmmm...' said King Ahab, who wasn't sure whether to believe Elijah or not.

Then God told Elijah to go and stay by a little stream.

'You can drink the water there and I will send birds to feed you.'

Elijah drank from the little stream. Every morning and every evening, birds came to Elijah, large black ravens, and brought him food to eat. And just as God had said, it stopped raining, and gradually Elijah's little stream dried up.

'Go now to the little village of Zarephath,' God told Elijah. 'There is a widow there who will make sure you have enough to eat.'

'It's all I have left,' the widow told Elijah. 'After this I have no more flour or oil to make bread.

But for as long as she shared her food with Elijah, God made sure that the little jar of flour and the little bottle of oil did not run out.

Fire on the mountain

There was still no rain. It was time for Elijah to go back to the King.

'What's going on?' grumbled King Ahab.

'Let's choose between the real God and the stone statue you call Baal,' said Elijah. 'We'll soon see who will send fire to cook a meal, and who will send rain again – the true and living God, or a god called Baal made of stone.'

Elijah laid a fire with wood on top of stones, ready to cook a meal. And the people who believed Baal was god laid a fire with wood on top of stones, ready to cook a meal.

'Come on, Baal!' shouted the people who worshipped the pretend god. 'Light our fire! Listen to us and answer! Listen to us! LISTEN TO US!'

They shouted and danced until they were exhausted and their throats were sore. But nothing happened.

'Has Baal run away?' teased Elijah. 'Perhaps he's gone to sleep? Perhaps he's on holiday!'

Elijah poured water all round his stones. Then he spoke to God.

'Let everyone see that you are the one true and living God,' prayed Elijah.

Then suddenly there was fire from heaven. The wood sizzled and the food on the fire sizzled. Then God sent the rain.

A dip in the river

Naaman was an important *soldier*, but he had *spots* and *blotches* and nasty sore places all over his *skin*.

A little servant girl lived with Naaman's wife. She wanted to help.

'There's a man in my own country who can make Naaman well again,' said the little girl. 'His name is Elisha. He is a prophet from God.'

So Naaman sent a message to the King in the servant girl's country.

'No good asking me,' the King said. 'I can't make you better. But you could go and visit Elisha.'

So Naaman went to visit Elisha.

'Go and wash in the River Jordan seven times,' said Elisha's servant.

Naaman wasn't very happy.

'First he sends his servant instead of seeing me himself. Then he tells me to have a bath! I thought he'd do something special – wave his arms, or say some prayers, or make me well straightaway! Grrrr!'

'Go on, Naaman,' said his friends. 'Just – do it!'

'Oh all right,' said Naaman crossly.

Grumpily, he went to the river. In he went.

Dip, dip, dip, dip, dip, dip, dip...

And the *spots* and *blotches* vanished.

'Wow!' said Naaman. 'It was all quite easy really when I did as I was told. Thank you, God! You really are special!'

Jonah runs the other way

God told Jonah to go to a city called Nineveh.

'The people there do a lot of wrong things,' said God.

But Jonah didn't want to go to Nineveh. So he ran away from God and sailed to a town called Joppa instead.

A big storm blew, and the sailors were afraid they'd all be drowned.

'Throw me into the sea!' said Jonah. 'It's all my fault! I've disobeyed God.'

'OK then,' said the sailors. 'If that's what you want.'

Immediately the sea became calm.

Then...

Gulpswallowgulp!

A seriously big fish swallowed Jonah.

It was rather dark inside.

Jonah stayed there for three days and three nights. He prayed to God.

Then...

Gulpgugglewoosh!

The seriously big fish tossed Jonah out of its mouth on to the beach. Jonah did as God had told him. He went to the city of Nineveh. He told the people there that they had done wrong things and that God would destroy their city.

Then the people said they were sorry, and God didn't destroy the city of Nineveh after all.

'I've wasted my time coming here,' sulked Jonah.

'But I'm glad my people are sorry for doing wrong things,' said God.

Daniel and the sound of music

Daniel was taken prisoner to the King's court in a place called Babylon, far away from home. He and his friends worshipped the one true God, but the King worshipped pretend gods.

One day, the King told everyone to bow down and worship a golden statue.

'I won't,' said Daniel's friend Shadrach.

'I won't,' said his friend Meshach.

'I won't,' said his friend Abednego.

'There'll be trouble if you don't!' said a messenger.

'As soon as you hear music and instruments, you'll bow down to that golden statue, or there'll be trouble – you wait and see! If you don't bow down and worship it – you'll be thrown into a fiery furnace!'

Daniel's friends still refused to worship the golden statue.

'We will only worship the one true God,' they said.

So they were thrown into the blazing fiery furnace. It was very, very, very hot.

But they did not die. They did not get burned. They didn't even smell smoky! God sent an angel into the fiery furnace to keep them safe. When the king brought them out of the fiery furnace, he knew that their God was the one true God!

Plots and plans and lions

The king's men didn't like Daniel because he was good and wise.

They were jealous of him. So they planned and plotted, they muttered and mumbled, they whispered and wittered, and they schemed skilfully, with their heads closely together.

'Anyone who thinks you're not the most special person on earth, oh King, shall be thrown to the lions,' they said, bowing low.

'OK!' said the King.

Daniel prayed to God every day at his open window.

The King's men saw him, and told the King.

'Daniel prays to God instead of to you,' they said.

'Daniel likes God best,' they said.

'Daniel doesn't worship you as he should,' they said.

'Daniel –'

'Ssh!' said the King. 'Enough!' The King wasn't very happy about throwing Daniel to the lions, but he had to do as he'd agreed.

'I hope your God will save you,' he said to Daniel as he sent him to the lions' den.

'GGGGGGGGGGGRRRRRRRRRRRR!'

The lions were hungry... and it was a long, lonely night for the King.

In the morning the King found Daniel... alive and well!

The lions padded about quietly.

'God took care of me,' said Daniel. 'I trusted him.'

'Daniel's God is a living God,' said the King in amazement. 'He will rule for ever!'

The promise of a king

'One day,' said God, 'the darkness and shadows will disappear. There'll be peace and joy and light, and a Kingdom of sunshine and happiness.

'A child will be born to us, a very special child. A son will be given to us, a very special son. There will be a Kingdom of peace – where wild animals and little children will rest together.

'Everyone,' continued God, 'everyone will know about love and truth and peace and joy.

'For a wonderful King is coming. Meanwhile... just wait. Just wait and see!'

A visitor for Mary

One day, a girl called Mary had a great surprise.

Mary was all on her own when an angel came to her. The angel's name was Gabriel.

'Don't be afraid,' said the angel Gabriel gently. 'I have a message for you from God. You are going to have a baby. The baby will be called Jesus, the Son of God.'

Mary was quite afraid but she was also very happy.

She ran to tell her cousin, Elizabeth, and they praised God together.

'I'm so happy,' Mary sang to God. 'You're wise and wonderful! 'You're the greatest and best!'

A ride to Bethlehem

It was nearly time for Mary's baby to be born. But Mary and Joseph had to travel a long way to Bethlehem.

When they reached the town, there were lots of visitors. There was nowhere for them to stay.

'No room!' said one innkeeper.

'No room!' said another.

'No room!' said yet one more.

All the inns were full of people. All the streets were full of people. All the town was full of people.

At last, one of the innkeepers

felt sorry for Mary and Joseph. He saw how tired they were. He could see that Mary's baby would soon be born.

'You can rest in the stable,' he said. And that night, Mary's baby was born, Jesus, the Son of God.

Mary wrapped him in cloth and made a bed for him in the manger where the animals feed.

The shepherds' surprise

That night, shepherds were out on the hills looking after their sheep. It was cold and quiet and dark... until suddenly... there was a bright light all around them! There was an angel with them! 'Don't be afraid,' said the angel. 'I've good news for you. Jesus,

the Son of God, is born in Bethlehem. You'll find him lying in a manger.'

Then lots more angels appeared: a sky full of angels!

'Glory to God!' they sang.

The shepherds rubbed their eyes... as the sky grew dark again. Whatever was happening?

They ran to Bethlehem, to see if it could be true – and there was the baby in the manger.

'Guess what happened?' said the shepherds to Mary and Joseph. 'There were angels... and guess what they said about this baby!'

With Joseph at her side, Mary thought hard about the angels' message, and the special baby lying in the manger. Then the shepherds went back to their sheep, praising God because his own Son had been born – and they had seen him!

Follow the star

A very bright star shone in the East, high in the sky.

Some wise men, who knew a lot about the stars, followed the very bright star. They knew it was a sign from God, a sign that would lead them to a new-born King.

They made a long, long journey, following the very bright star all the way, to find the new-born King.

'We will bring him gifts fit for a King,' they said.

'I will bring him gold,' said one.

'I will bring him frankincense,' said another.

'I will bring him myrrh,' said a third.

They travelled on, and on... and on... and on... all the time following the very bright star, until at last the wise men found Jesus with Mary, his mother.

They knelt down in wonder and

gave him their gifts of gold, frankincense and myrrh. They worshipped Jesus, the Son of God.

Then the wise men travelled home again, to their lands in the East.

Jesus gets lost

Jesus was growing up.

Every year, he went to the temple in Jerusalem with his mother, Mary, and with Joseph for a special festival called the Passover.

When Jesus was twelve years old, Jesus got lost...

As usual there were crowds of people there. As usual Mary and Joseph left Jerusalem with everyone else.

After a time, Mary said:

'Where's Jesus?'

'I think he's with those people over there,' said Joseph, looking. But they couldn't find Jesus anywhere!

'Jesus, where are you?' called Mary and Joseph.

They called his name and asked and looked everywhere, but still they couldn't find Jesus! So Mary and Joseph went back to Jerusalem.

They found him in the temple

listening to the teachers. 'Where have you *been*?' asked Mary anxiously.

'We've been very worried about you!' said Joseph. 'Are you playing hide-and-seek with us?'

'I was quite all right,' said Jesus. 'You shouldn't have come to look for me. I needed to *be* in God's house – my Father's house – so I could learn all about him.'

Jesus went back home with Mary and Joseph and grew taller and stronger, and went on learning about God.

Jesus is baptised

A man called John lived in the wild desert. He wore rough, hairy clothes and he ate insects and honey.

John told all the people that a very special person, Jesus, the Messiah, was coming.

'Make way for him, make way!' said John. 'God is sending us a king. You must be sorry for all the wrong things you've ever done and be baptised as a sign that God is washing you clean.'

Then, one day, Jesus himself came and asked John to baptise him, too, in the River Jordan.

John was surprised. He realised that Jesus was the special king that God had

promised. John *believed* that Jesus was the Messiah.
John knew that Jesus, who had *been* born in a stable,
was the Son of God.

 Jesus hadn't done anything wrong. But
John did as Jesus asked. He baptised him.

 As Jesus came up out of the water,
John saw a dove fluttering around
above Jesus' head. He heard
God's voice speaking
from heaven.

 'This is my Son,'
said God.

The Lord's Prayer

Jesus told people how to pray to God.

'God loves to hear his children pray to him,' said Jesus. 'But don't use long words that don't mean much. Be honest with God. Tell him what you really feel.'

Then Jesus gave them a pattern to use to help them. People all over the world say this prayer. They call it 'The Lord's Prayer'.

'Our Father in heaven,

'Your name is great and holy.

'We want to do what is right, so that your love will spread all over the world.

'Please give everyone enough to eat each day, and help us to be kind to each other always.

'Keep us safe from harm and from doing wrong things.

'For you are true and wonderful and glorious and your kingdom
will last for ever and ever and ever. Amen.'

God cares about you

'Don't worry too much about your food and drink and clothes,' said Jesus.

'Look at the birds and the flowers. Our heavenly Father God cares for the birds and they all find food.

'And look how the wild flowers grow. God has made them look beautiful. They're as fine and colourful as a King's clothes.

'God gives us all we need when we love him and trust him and share with each other. Then there will be enough food and drink and clothes for everyone.'

Later, Jesus watched some sparrows as the tiny birds flew and hopped about and pecked at the ground.

'God knows and cares for everyone, even the tiniest of these sparrows,' said Jesus. 'God is great and mighty and powerful but he knows every little bird. A little sparrow doesn't seem very important, but God knows if one falls to the ground. He knows us and cares for each one of us, too. We needn't be afraid if we know we're safe in his strong, Kind hands.'

Very special friends

Jesus needed twelve very special friends. He wanted them to go everywhere with him and help him in his work: telling people all about God; making ill people feel better; making *bad* people want to *be good*; making *sad* people happy and smiley again.

Jesus called to four fishermen, Peter, Andrew, James and John. They were busy with their nets beside the sea.

'Hello there!' called Jesus. 'Leave your nets, and come and follow me!' And they did.

Later on, Jesus met Matthew. No one liked him much. He sat counting his money.

'Hello there!' said Jesus. 'Leave your money, and come and follow me!' And Matthew did.

Jesus asked God to help him choose the right people to be his friends. Here they all are:

Peter, Andrew, James, John, Philip, Bartholomew, Matthew, Thomas, James (yes, there were two!), Thaddeus, Simon, Judas.

Can you count them...?

Altogether there were twelve very special friends.

Sometimes they went out two by two by two, telling everyone some very good news.

'God loves you!' they said. 'God is great!'

'God wants you to love him and be happy.'

'God wants you to love other people, and to be part of his special kingdom.'

Wine at the wedding

Jesus went with his mother Mary and his friends to a wedding. It was a happy time, with talking and laughing, family and friends and fun. There were lots of good things to eat and drink – until suddenly there was no wine left! It had all run out! There was nothing left to drink but water!

Mary spoke to Jesus.

'There's no wine left,' she said. 'Please do something! Please help – or the party will be spoiled for everyone!'

'Fill the jars with water,' Jesus said to the servants. 'Fill them right up to the top, then take the water to the guests.'

The servants did exactly what Jesus told them – then something extraordinary happened. As it was poured, the water turned into clear, beautiful wine, flowing brightly.

Jesus' friends watched in amazement. Their eyes opened wider and wider. So did the eyes of the host at the wedding party when he tasted the wine.

'My goodness!' he said. 'What a surprise! Thank you for keeping this wine until now. It's wonderful wine! It's the best!'

Jesus' disciples were astonished.

'Jesus is wonderful and special,' they said. 'He makes everyone happy.'

The hole in the roof

Jesus was in town!

And so was a man who couldn't walk. He lay on a mattress until his four kind friends carried him to Jesus.

But they found a HUGE crowd of people filling the house. They couldn't get into the house. They couldn't get near the house. They couldn't *see* Jesus at all!

Then the four friends had a good idea. They clambered and climbed and carried their friend on to the top of the house.

They scrabbled and scraped at the roof until they made a little hole. Dust and earth fell and flew everywhere until the hole grew bigger... and bigger... and *so* big that they could let their friend down into the house – right at Jesus' feet.

'Well, hello there,' said Jesus.

Jesus told the man he would forgive him for anything he'd ever done wrong. Some of the people were grumbly.

'Who does Jesus think he is?' they muttered.

Others were astonished. All were amazed!

Then Jesus said to the man:

'Pick up your mattress, and walk home.'

And he did!

'We've never seen anything like this!' said all the people, and they praised God.

The story of two houses

Jesus once told a story about two men and two houses.

'I think I'll build a house,' said the first man, who was sensible and wise.

'I'll build it over there on that good strong rock. That rock looks good and solid and safe. It will be a very nice house indeed.'

The first man's house was a very fine house when it was finished. Its dark little windows looked out at the rock on which it was built, good and solid and safe. It was a very fine house indeed.

'I'm going to build a house, too,' said the second man, who was foolish and silly.

'But I'm going to build mine over there on the sand. Rocks are dull and boring. My house will be on a beautiful, wide golden beach.'

The second man's house was a very fine house when it was finished. Its dark little windows looked out at the sand on which it was built, on a beautiful, wide golden beach. It was a very fine house indeed.

The house that fell down

One day there was a great storm. The rain rained – pitter-patter.

The rivers rose – higher and higher. The wind whistled – whoooooooo!

The first man sat in his fine house and heard the great storm rumble and clatter and blow around him.

'I'm surrounded by slushy, sloshing storms!' he said. 'My roof is rustling, my door is dripping and drowning. My shelves are shaking – but... I'm standing firm and dry, safe and sound on my strong foundations! My house is built on the hard and solid rock!'

The second man sat in his fine house and heard the great storm rumble and clatter and blow around him.

'My windows are windy, my walls are weak and wobbling, my floors are falling in, my upstairs is downstairs and my stones are sliding into the slippery sand – Ohhhhhhhhhhhhhhhh!'

'Which is wiser?' asked Jesus. 'To build on rock or to build on sand? Listen well to this story. Make sure your life is built on the solid rock of my words, which are true and strong and will not tumble around your ears when troubles come.'

The storm at sea

Jesus and his friends were out in a boat on the lake. Everywhere was very quiet and still.

Soon, Jesus fell asleep. It had been a long day and he was very tired.

Then... suddenly... there was a big storm!

'Whoooooooooooooo!' blew the wind.

'Crash! Splash! Wisshh! Whoosh!' washed the waves.

Some of the waves blew into the boat. The wind tossed the boat up and down, up and down.

But Jesus stayed fast asleep.

Jesus' friends were very afraid.

'Wake up!' they said to Jesus. 'Wake up! WAKE UP!'

Jesus woke up. He stood up. He spoke to the wind.

'Hush... be quiet,' said Jesus. And the wind was quiet.

Then Jesus spoke to the waves.

'Hush... calm down,' said Jesus. And the waves were calm.

The wind and the waves both did as Jesus told them. Everywhere became calm... and quiet... and still...

Jesus' friends weren't afraid now. Their wonderful friend Jesus had calmed the storm!

Little Miss Jairus

Little Miss Jairus wasn't very well. She lay in bed feeling tired and aching and poorly. She felt so unwell that Mr Jairus, her daddy, went to find Jesus.

'I know he can help us,' said Mr Jairus. 'Jesus helps everybody.'

And that day, everybody did want Jesus to help them. There were crowds of people everywhere. They pushed and pulled and shouted and shoved and jiggled and jostled and poked and prodded at Jesus. So it took Jesus a long time to reach Mr Jairus' house.

His friends, Peter and James and John, went with him. When at last they reached the house everyone was wailing and crying and sad.

'You're too late, Jesus,' they sobbed.

'Stop crying,' said Jesus. 'She's only asleep.'

Then Mr and Mrs Jairus and Peter and James and John watched. Jesus took the girl's hands and said:

'Get up, little girl! Wake up! Stand up!'

And little Miss Jairus did get up! She woke up! She stood up! She was well again!

And to everyone else Jesus said:

'Cheer up! Jump up! Hurry up! She's hungry! Find her something to eat.'

Then Mr Jairus and Mrs Jairus and Little Miss Jairus were very, very happy that Jesus had made her better and well again.

The enormous picnic

What a big picnic!

Just look at all those people eating a picnic out on the hillside. There are THOUSANDS of them!

Lots of people had been with Jesus. They heard him tell stories. They heard him talk about God as if he really knew what he was like. They saw him make blind people see and ill people better. The people would follow Jesus anywhere.

By evening everyone was hungry but – oh dear! – they were too far from home and there was nothing to eat.

Then a little boy came to Jesus with all he had. He gave it to Jesus and his friends, just five flat little bread rolls and two little fishes that his mother had given him. The boy shared all he had with Jesus.

'Thank you, God, for all you give us,' said Jesus, looking up.

Then the disciples shared out the food until suddenly everybody had enough to eat. It was a very, very big and happy picnic.

There were even twelve baskets of food left over. Jesus' friends tidied them all up before everyone went home.

The story of the good Samaritan

'How can I show God that I love him?' a man once asked Jesus. 'Love God as well as you are able, and look after other people as if you loved them too,' Jesus replied. Then Jesus told a story so the man knew what he meant.

'There was a man who'd been walking from one town to another, when he was beaten and robbed.

'The man lay by the side of the road. He hurt all over. He felt sick and very sad.

'Then the man heard footsteps in the distance coming nearer... louder... and then going away, softly... softly... on the other side of the road.

'Then the man heard more footsteps in the distance coming nearer... louder... and going away, softly... softly... on the other side of the road.

'Then the man heard clippetty-clop, clippetty-clop, a man on a donkey, a man from another country that people didn't like: a stranger, an enemy!

'But the stranger bathed his wounds, helped him on to his donkey and took him to an inn to rest. The kind stranger paid the innkeeper to go on taking care of him, until he was well enough to leave. Although he had been a stranger, he had looked after him as if he really cared about him.'

Trouble in the kitchen

Jesus went to Mary and Martha's house for supper.
Mary liked listening to Jesus. She sat quietly at his feet.
He had so many wonderful stories to tell. He had so many

wonderful things to talk about. He had so many wonderful things to teach.

Martha liked listening to Jesus too. But she was busy, getting the meal ready. There was so much work to do: tidying and clearing up, cooking and stirring, mashing and mixing, chopping and peeling, whisking and washing. Some things were bubbling and boiling when they shouldn't be. Some things weren't doing anything at all that they should be.

'Oh dear, oh dear, oh DEAR!' thought Martha, growing more and more hot and flustered. This meal would never be ready for Jesus!

'I've all this work to do on my own!' grumbled Martha to Jesus. 'Can't you tell Mary to come and help?'

Jesus smiled. 'Don't be so worried, Martha,' said Jesus kindly. 'Just come and sit down with me. It can all wait. We'll have supper later when it's all ready.'

The story of the lost sheep

'God loves you like a good shepherd loves his sheep!' Jesus once said. Then he told a story.

'Once there was a shepherd who had 100 sheep. But one of the sheep went off wandering. It nibbled juicy grass.

'"I'm happy," said the little sheep. "Baa-ha."

'The little sheep wandered off further.
It nibbled juicy grass, and skipped and ran.

'"I'm so happy," said the little sheep. "Baa-ha."

'The little sheep wandered further and further. It nibbled juicy grass, and skipped and ran over the hills and far away.

'Then... the little sheep wandered further and further and further. It grew dark and cold. There wasn't any more juicy grass, only rocky hills and prickly bushes.

'"I'm sad and lonely," said the little sheep. "I want to go home. I'm tired. I'm hungry. I'm lost! Please will somebody come and find me."

'And somebody did. The shepherd counted his sheep.

'97... 98... 99... There was one missing! He left his other sheep and clambered over the hillside, shouting and searching, climbing and calling... until at last he found his little lost sheep and carried him safely in his arms down the steep rocky path.

'"I'm really happy I've found you," said the shepherd. "Let's have a party! Let's celebrate!"'

The story of the loving father

'Good loves you,' said Jesus. 'God loves you so much, he waits until you are ready to say you have made a mistake and come back to him to say sorry. God is like the father in this story. 'The father had two sons. The younger son ran away from

home taking his share of his father's money. Suddenly he was rich! He spent and spent and spent his money on all sorts of things – until suddenly he'd spent it all!

'Now he didn't have any money left. He was poor. He was so poor that he had to go and work very hard on a pig farm. He was so poor that he felt very, very hungry. He was so poor that he ate the pigs' food. He was so poor and hungry that he decided to go home to his father.

'His father saw him coming from a long way away. He was overjoyed to see him. He hugged him and kissed him.

'"I'm really sorry," said the young man to his father. "I've done everything wrong to you and to my family and to God. I've been selfish and greedy and..."

'But his father was already calling to his servants.

'"He's come home!" he shouted. "My son's home again! Bring his best cloak, and a ring for his finger and shoes for his feet. Let's celebrate! Let's have a feast! Let's have music and dancing! Let the party begin!"'

The man who couldn't see

Bartimaeus was blind. He couldn't see anything at all.

He couldn't see the flowers – although he could smell them.

He couldn't see the trees – although he could hear the wind rustle their leaves, and feel the rough bark of their trunks when he sat under their shade.

He couldn't see the blue sky and white wispy clouds – although he could feel the hot sun and the cool breeze.

He couldn't see the people around him – although he could hear their voices laughing and shouting and joking and playing.

Bartimaeus was blind, and because he could not see he could not work. Because Bartimaeus could not work, he could not eat! So he sat by the roadside, day after day, calling out to people, begging them for money.

Bartimaeus' eyes were dark and sad.

Help me!

One day, Bartimaeus heard people coming along the road. He heard the sound of their feet and knew it was a large crowd. He heard the sound of their voices and knew it was a happy crowd.

When Bartimaeus asked and found out that Jesus was coming, he called out too.

'Jesus!' called Bartimaeus. 'Help me!'

'Sssssssssssshhhhh!' said everybody, shocked.

So Bartimaeus called out again, more loudly, this time.

'HELP ME!'

'Sssssssssssshhhhh!' said everybody again, even more shocked.

'Who's there?' said Jesus.

'It's me, and I want to see,' said Bartimaeus. 'Please!'

Kind hands helped him to his feet and Kind hands led him to Jesus.

'Go along and you'll be well,' said Jesus gently. 'You shall see.'

Bartimaeus opened his eyes – wider... wider... and yes! He could see!

He could see the flowers. He could see the trees. He could see the sky and the clouds, and he could see all the people smiling at him. He could see everything!

He could see Jesus, too, and so Bartimaeus followed him along the road.

'Thank you, God!' said Bartimaeus.

'Praise God!' said everyone.

The man who climbed a tree

Once there was a little man called Zacchaeus. He was very rich, and had a lot of money. He'd not always been a kind man or a good man and he didn't have many friends. In fact, he didn't really have any friends. People said he was a cheat.

Zacchaeus was very small. He wanted to see Jesus, who was coming along the road. But so did lots of other people. And Zacchaeus couldn't see over their heads. Then he had a good idea.

He climbed into the branches of a fig tree – and looked down on all the people. He knew Jesus would come soon...

At last, here was Jesus. He looked up – and saw Zacchaeus looking down at him!

'Come down,' said Jesus to Zacchaeus. 'Come on, hurry down. I want to come to your house today.'

Zacchaeus slithered down through the branches as fast as a grown man could.

He took Jesus home to tea. Soon he was telling Jesus that he was sorry for the wrong things he'd done.

'You're my friend now,' said Zacchaeus to Jesus. 'I'll give money back to anyone I have cheated, and share what I have left with the poor.' Then Zacchaeus felt very, very happy.

Jesus rides a donkey

Jesus and his friends were on their way to the big city of Jerusalem.

'There's a new little donkey over in that village,' Jesus said to his friends one day. 'It's never been ridden before. I need that donkey. It's young and wild, but untie it and bring it to me.'

Carefully, Jesus' special friends fetched the donkey. They put their cloaks over the donkey's back and helped Jesus to climb on.

Jesus rode on along the road to Jerusalem. It was all very noisy and exciting. Crowds of people followed him. Lots of men, lots of women, lots of children followed too.

They threw their cloaks down on the road in front of him. They threw palm branches down on the road in front of him. They cheered and waved and shouted. They jostled and pushed to see the procession.

'Hurrah!' everyone cried out.
'Praise God! Hosanna!
'Praise the King of peace!
'Praise King Jesus!'

Less but more

One day, Jesus and his friends were near the temple together. They watched people coming and going and dropping money into a box. Some rich people put a lot of money in. They made sure people were looking as they put LOTS of money in the box.

Then a poor woman came along. She had no husband and very little money. She didn't look to see who was watching. She didn't care what people thought of her at all. She came because she loved God. That was all.

Quietly, she dropped two little coins into the box. 'Look,' said Jesus to his disciples. 'This widow woman has been really generous.

'The rich people gave a lot. But the rich are rich. They still have lots of money left. This woman has hardly enough to eat. She has given everything she has. So what the widow gave may be less money but she has given far more.'

A lonely garden

Jesus had a special meal with his friends. They ate bread and drank wine together. Jesus told them to remember that special night every time they ate bread and drank wine in the future.

Then they went out into a dark, quiet garden.

Jesus prayed to God.

'I will do whatever you want,' said Jesus. 'But please help me, Father.'

Jesus was sad because Judas, one of his special friends, didn't want to be his friend any more. He was going to give Jesus to his enemies who would be cruel and hurt him.

The disciples were tired. They couldn't keep their eyes open a moment longer. They all fell asleep.

Jesus felt sad and lonely.

'Wake up!' Jesus said to them. 'Look what's happening.'

Suddenly, there was light and noise. Torches and flares were blazing. Swords were clashing, rough voices shouting.

Then one of Jesus friends stepped out of the darkness. He kissed Jesus, pretending to be kind. It was Judas.

Then the soldiers knew.

'That's him!' said a voice.

'Here he is!' said another voice.

'Get him!' said one.

'Grab him!' said another.

And the soldiers took Jesus away.

Three crosses

On a lonely hill, Jesus was killed. He was crucified on a cross between two other crosses.

Three crosses – a thief, a robber and between them, Jesus, God's Son, who had given the blind their sight, given the deaf their hearing, loved them, helped them, and made them well.

Jesus asked his Father God to forgive the soldiers and the thieves and everyone in the world for everything they'd ever done wrong.

Then there was an earthquake. There was darkness in the middle of the day. The curtain in the temple was torn in two.

The sun went down and Jesus died.

It was the saddest day there had ever, ever been.

A sad garden

A good man called Joseph, and another man Jesus had helped called Nicodemus, carried Jesus' body to his own beautiful garden.

Scents of flowers and damp grass and leafy trees drifted across the dewy evening air. The garden felt grey and quiet and still.

They buried Jesus in a quiet, dark cave. Then they pushed a very big, heavy stone across

the doorway.

No one could get in. No one could get out. That was that.

Jesus' mother was very sad. Jesus' friend John was very sad. They looked after each other. All Jesus' friends were very, very sad. They knew they would never see Jesus again.

It was the quietest day there had ever, ever been.

A happy garden

Early on Sunday morning, the women took their sweet-smelling spices to the garden where Jesus was buried.

But when they reached the place, they found that the big, heavy stone had been rolled away and the tomb was empty.

Two shining angels sat beside the cave.

'Jesus isn't here,' said the angel. 'Go and tell everyone – he is alive again!'

The women wept for joy! They ran to tell Peter and Jesus' other friends, but they could not understand what had happened.

Peter and John ran to the garden – and saw the empty tomb for themselves, but they could not understand what had happened.

Mary Magdalene stayed by the empty cave, crying. She could not understand what had happened.

'Why are you crying?' said a voice behind her.

'They've taken Jesus away,' she wept. 'Have you taken him away? Where have you put him?'

As Mary turned to look at the man, she realised that it was

Jesus! Mary couldn't believe her eyes. She was so, so happy.

The sun rose and the birds sang. Mary ran back to Peter and Jesus' other friends and told them – 'Jesus is alive!'

It was the happiest day there had ever, ever been.

Two friends along the road

That very same evening, a man called Cleopas and his friend were walking to a nearby village. They talked together quietly and sadly, because Jesus had died.

Suddenly, a stranger joined them.

'Why are you so sad?' asked the stranger.

'We're sad because Jesus has died,' said the two friends.

'He was to be our King, but now he's been killed.'

Then they all went on their way together, Cleopas, his friend, and the stranger.

He talked and they listened. He told them
wonderful, exciting things about God.

'Come in and have supper with us,' said the friends
when they reached Emmaus. 'It's getting late and dark.'

The stranger broke some bread

– and suddenly the friends knew
who he was. It was Jesus!

Then, just as suddenly...
he wasn't there any more...

'We knew he was
someone special,' said
Cleopas.

'We felt warm and
happy when he talked to us,'
said Cleopas' friend.

'Quick, quick!' they said.
'We must go and tell the
others! Jesus really is alive!'

Jesus and Thomas

Yes, Jesus really was alive again.

One day, when his special friends were all together, Jesus slipped into the room, although the door was firmly shut.

'Peace be with you,' said Jesus.

The disciples' eyes opened wider and wider. Their mouths opened wider and wider. They were astonished at seeing Jesus again.

Could it really be Jesus?

'Don't be afraid,' said Jesus kindly. 'It really is me, your friend. Look at my hands and feet. You can see where I was hurt. Now, what about some fish for supper?'

Thomas had not been with the others. He couldn't believe that Jesus was alive again, walking and talking with people, and eating fish for supper!

'But it's true,' said his friends. 'We've seen him. We've spoken to him. Jesus really is alive!'

The next time Jesus slipped into the room, Thomas was there too.

'Peace be with you,' said Jesus again. 'Look at me,' Jesus said to Thomas. 'Look at me and touch me. There's no doubt it's me!'

Thomas looked... and looked... and looked again...and then he knew that it was Jesus.

'Jesus!' gasped Thomas. 'It really is you. You are my Lord.'

Breakfast on the shore

One night, Peter and his friends were out in their boat, fishing on Lake Galilee.

They fished and fished and fished all night, but they didn't catch any fish at all.

Just as the sun was rising, they heard a man's voice from the water's edge.

'Have you caught anything?' called the man.

'No, nothing,' they replied gloomily. 'Not even the tiniest, teeniest, tiddliest tiddler.'

'Try again,' the man shouted back to them. 'Put out your net on the other side.'

'Come on, lads,' sighed Peter. 'One more go. Heave-ho.'

So the friends heaved and hoed and put out their net on the other side of the boat.

Suddenly the net was full of big fish, so many fish that the friends could hardly pull the net in! Then they knew who the man on the shore must be.

'It's Jesus!' they said.

Peter jumped into the water and waded to the beach. And there was Jesus, making breakfast.

The friends dragged in the net, full of wiggling, wriggling fish.

'Come and eat,' said Jesus, and they all ate fish and bread together on the beach.

After breakfast, Jesus gave Peter a special task.

'Always follow me,' said Jesus, 'and take care of all my friends for me.'

Jesus goes to heaven

Jesus and his special friends stood talking to each other on a high hillside.

'Will you soon be our real King?' his friends asked Jesus.

'Not quite yet,' smiled Jesus kindly. 'One day. I'm going back to heaven first. I'm going back to God. But I want you to tell other people all about me. I want you to tell other people how they can be happy. I want you to tell other people that the secret of being happy is to love God and be kind to everyone else. I will always be with you to help you.'

Then Jesus asked God to bless his friends and love them.

As he spoke, a cloud came down the hillside. When the cloud moved away, Jesus had vanished.

His friends stared and stared up at the clear sky.

Then two angels stood beside them.

'Don't go on looking at the sky,' said the angels. 'One day, Jesus will come back again.'

Wind and fire

Jesus' special friends were all together on a special feast day called Pentecost.

Then... suddenly... there was a wind, a strong wind, a strong and mighty wind, a strong and mighty rushing wind, a strong and mighty rushing wind that filled the whole house.

'WHOOOOOO!'

And then... suddenly... there were little flames, safe, bright little flames that didn't burn, but touched everyone's heads.

'Wow!' said everyone, feeling very excited and happy. 'Let's praise God! Let's tell God how much we love him! He's filling us up with his love! We can talk in other languages! We can understand other languages! We can tell everyone about our friend Jesus, about how special he is and how much he wants everyone to be his friend.'

A big crowd gathered outside the house.

'Whatever's going on?' said the people in the crowd.

'They're drunk! They're talking rubbish and drivel and nonsense!'

Then Peter stood up and told the people all about the Lord Jesus, who was God's Son, come to save them.

'God's Spirit has come,' he said. 'It's as if Jesus himself were back here with us, promising that he will always be with us to help us in all we do.'

Power at Pentecost

God helped Peter and John and his other friends to be bold and brave. He helped them to be powerful and peaceful.

Peter spoke to all the crowds of people.

'Jesus is God's Son,' said Peter. 'He loves you and died for you. He is the Lord and King. You must stop doing wrong things and he will forgive you.'

A lot of people listened to Peter together. They learned about God together. They prayed and praised together. They had meals together. They cared and shared together.

God helped them make ill people well again. Jesus' friends weren't afraid any more. They knew that God was always with them, although he was invisible, like the wind.

A new name

A man called Saul loved God, but hated all the new Christians.

'Bah! Stupid! You're all wrong. Go away!' he said.

One day, Saul was going along a road to a city called Damascus. While he was there, he planned to stop people following Jesus.

Suddenly, there was a bright light all around Saul. The light was so bright that Saul couldn't see, and he fell to the ground. Then Saul heard a voice.

It was Jesus!

'When you're cruel to the people who love me, you're being cruel to me too,' said Jesus.

After that Saul became quite different. He wanted Jesus to be his friend. He wanted to be a Christian, too.

'I'm such a different person. I want to have a different name,' said Saul. 'My new name is going to be Paul.'

Paul joined the Christians and shared the work of telling everyone about Jesus. He was just as keen to help them as he had been to stop them. News spread everywhere about God's love and forgiveness and soon people in many places were baptised and started to follow and worship Jesus.

Peter in prison

Peter told everyone about how much God loved them. He told them that Jesus had died and risen again so that everyone could be God's friends and live with him in heaven one day.

But there were people who didn't like what Peter said. Peter was put in prison and chained up between two guards.

'Let's pray for Peter,' said Peter's friends one night. Together, in Mary's house, they prayed to God. Meanwhile, Peter was sleeping peacefully in prison.

Suddenly, there was an angel there with Peter and the prison

cell was full of light!

'Wake up!' said the angel. 'Get dressed and follow me.'

The chains fell from Peter's wrists and he followed the angel out of the prison. The prison guards didn't notice him, and the big iron gates swung open for him. Peter went straight to Mary's house where all his friends were gathered.

Knock, knock, knock! Peter knocked on the door.

A little girl called Rhoda answered.

'It's Peter! It's Peter!' she shouted. She was so excited, she forgot to let him in!

Knock, knock, knock! Peter tried again.

This time everyone rushed to the door. When his friends saw it really was Peter, they praised God. He had answered their prayers.

Shipwreck!

Paul and his friends had many adventures. They travelled a lot and made many journeys to tell people all about Jesus.

Sometimes their journeys were dangerous. Sometimes their journeys were long. Sometimes they travelled by sea.

Sometimes Paul was put in prison.

'I want to go to Rome to see the emperor,' decided Paul. 'He's important and fair and I'm sure he'll let me stay out of prison. Then I can go on telling people about the Lord Jesus.'

So Paul and his friends sailed to Rome.

At first the sea was calm, but then the wind blew harder! The ship rocked and tipped up and down, up and down in the big waves. But God took care of Paul and his friends.

'God will look after us. We won't drown,' said Paul. And they didn't drown.

At last, the boat was wrecked just off the island of Malta. People there welcomed the shipwrecked sailors, and looked after them until it was safe for them to sail again to Rome.

Then Paul was allowed to stay in a house and write to all his friends, teaching them about Jesus, even though he was a long way from them.

Paul writes
some thank-you letters

Paul wrote letters to Christians in some of the places he had visited.

He wrote to tell them that he often thought about them and asked God to look after them.

He wrote to thank them for making him welcome.

He wrote to tell them that God loved them so much that he had sent Jesus to help them.

He wrote to remind them that none of them were perfect and they all needed God's forgiveness.

He wrote to remind them to love God, not just today but every day.

He wrote to remind them to be kind to each other, and to share what they had with other people.

At the end of one of his letters he wrote:

'God is great and full of glory for ever!'

No more tears

After Jesus had risen from the dead, a man called John, who loved God very much, was sent to live on an island in the middle of the sea. The island was called Patmos.

While he was there, he wrote to some other people who loved God, and this is what he said:

'God is pure, and God is holy.

'God is good, and God is true and fair.

'Holy, holy, holy is the Lord God Almighty.

'He will live and reign for ever.

'All the angels and every creature will worship him for ever and ever.'

Then the man called John heard loud trumpets in the starry skies. He saw a sparkling, flowing river and tree-

lined streets. He imagined a wonderful heavenly city shining like the sun.

It was a holy city, where there would be no more hurts and pains, no more dying and no more crying. It was a wonderful city, and everyone who lived there could see God living among them – and God would wipe away every tear from their eyes.

'Lord Jesus, come and be with everyone,' said John.

Bible stories can be found as follows:

God made the world Genesis 1:1-31

Noah builds a boat Genesis 7:1 – 8:22

Under the stars Genesis 12:1-5; 15:5-6

Three visitors Genesis 18:1-15; 21:1

Isaac and Rebecca Genesis 24:1-66

Joseph and his brothers Genesis 37:1-36

Dreams come true Genesis 41:1 – 47:12

Little baby Moses Exodus 2:1-10

The king who said 'No!' Exodus 3:1 – 12:32

Follow-my-leader Exodus 16:1-18; 17:1-7; 19:1-21

The best way to live Exodus 20:1-17

Joshua's big battle Joshua 6:1-21

Gideon's good friend, God Judges 6:11 – 7:25

Ruth in the cornfield Ruth 1:1 – 4:13

The voice in the night 1 Samuel 1:1-28; 3:1-10

Seven sons and a shepherd boy 1 Samuel 16:1-13

David and Goliath 1 Samuel 17:17-50

David the song-writer Psalm 23:1-6

Solomon 1 Kings 3:1-14

Elijah and the ravens 1 Kings 17:1-16

Fire on the mountain 1 Kings 18:20-39

A dip in the river 2 Kings 5:1-14

Jonah runs the other way Jonah 1:1 – 3:10

Daniel and the sound of music Daniel 3:1-30

Plots and plans and lions Daniel 6:1-27

The promise of a King Isaiah 9:6-7; 11:6-9

A visitor for Mary Luke 1:26-55

A ride to Bethlehem Luke 2:1-7

The shepherds' surprise Luke 2:8-20

Follow the star Matthew 2:1-12

Jesus gets lost Luke 2:41-51

Jesus is baptised Matthew 3:1-6, 13-17

The Lord's Prayer Matthew 6:5-13

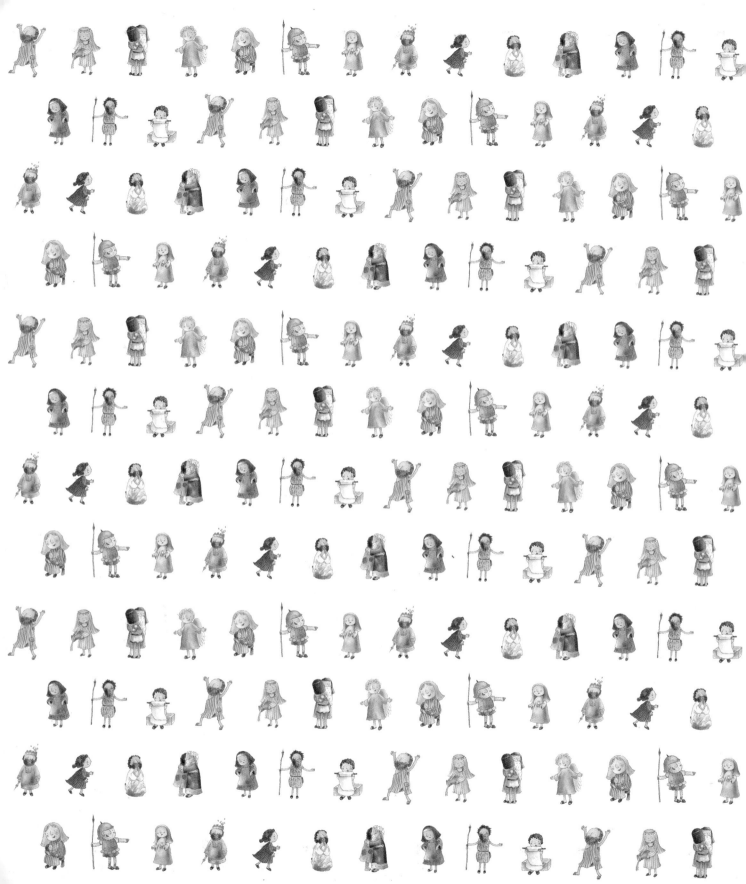